# Triple Muse

# TRIPLE MUSE

## JOHN ZEDOLIK

RESOURCE *Publications* · Eugene, Oregon

TRIPLE MUSE

Copyright © 2025 John Zedolik. All rights reserved. Except for brief quotations in critical publications or reviews, no part of this book may be reproduced in any manner without prior written permission from the publisher. Write: Permissions, Wipf and Stock Publishers, 199 W. 8th Ave., Suite 3, Eugene, OR 97401.

Resource Publications
An Imprint of Wipf and Stock Publishers
199 W. 8th Ave., Suite 3
Eugene, OR 97401

www.wipfandstock.com

PAPERBACK ISBN: 979-8-3852-6387-5
HARDCOVER ISBN: 979-8-3852-6388-2
EBOOK ISBN: 979-8-3852-6389-9

VERSION NUMBER 12/01/25

# Contests

## Observations:

| | |
|---|---|
| Elevation | 1 |
| Road and Crew | 2 |
| Unequal Opportunity Employer | 3 |
| Account for Average Wear | 4 |
| Trust | 5 |
| Private Composition | 6 |
| Thin Tally | 7 |
| Integration | 8 |
| Sharp Eye | 9 |
| Low Matter | 10 |
| Already Worked Out | 11 |
| Short Break | 12 |
| Agreeable Empyrean | 13 |
| Exceptional Moment | 14 |
| Peeve | 15 |
| Turnover | 16 |
| Spun Gold | 17 |
| Grounded | 18 |
| Final Significance | 19 |
| Telling Take | 20 |
| Animal Instincts | 22 |
| No Bother | 23 |
| Possible Improvement | 24 |
| Spot Assessment | 25 |
| Capable Span | 26 |
| Squamous Serenity | 28 |
| Reestablishment | 29 |
| Pharos | 30 |
| Refreshing Verisimilitude | 31 |
| Transaction | 32 |
| Inundation | 34 |
| The Inalienable | 35 |
| Current Vacuum | 36 |
| Sea Wrack | 37 |
| Dear Psyche | 38 |
| Pension | 39 |
| Good and Services | 40 |
| Noted | 41 |
| Casual Glance | 42 |
| Total Recall | 43 |
| Proper Maintenance | 44 |
| Safe Inside | 45 |

## Recollections:

| | |
|---|---|
| Equipoise | 47 |
| The Trend Set | 49 |
| Short-Sighted Super | 50 |
| Shared Experience | 51 |

| | | | |
|---|---|---|---|
| Capacities | 53 | Egalitarian Outcome | 85 |
| Score | 55 | Charged Atmosphere | 86 |
| Fluid Situation | 56 | At Liberty | 87 |
| Gentle Reminder | 57 | Divergence | 88 |
| Projector | 59 | Leeway | 89 |
| Blues Cast | 60 | Heated Overstatement | 90 |
| Progressive Infusion | 61 | Deep Challenge | 91 |
| A Portion of Success | 62 | Transferable Skill | 92 |
| Strike | 64 | | |
| Work Related | 66 | **Ruminations:** | |
| Firm Realization | 68 | Hope for the Season | 93 |
| Held Over | 69 | In Trust | 94 |
| Uncertain License | 71 | Fabric to Mend | 95 |
| Nary a Thought | 72 | Fugitive Relief | 96 |
| Logical Application | 74 | Blocks | 97 |
| Conjurers | 75 | Tour | 98 |
| B.Y.O. Exclusion | 76 | Charge Into | 99 |
| Wanderlust | 77 | Framed Declaration | 100 |
| Rival Faith | 78 | Simple Symposium | 101 |
| Potential Conflagration | 80 | Critical Eye | 102 |
| Facial Recognition | 81 | In Perpetuity | 103 |
| Caution Close | 82 | Former Integrity | 104 |
| Stopgap | 83 | Open Letter | 105 |
| Service, No Shoes | 84 | | |

# Acknowledgments

"Elevation," "Road and Crew," and "Equipoise," in *Home Planet News Online: An Independent Literary Review*, Issue #9, High Falls, NY (November 2021)

"The Trend Set" and "Unequal Opportunity Employer" in *Loch Raven Review*, Volume 18, Number 1, Baltimore, MD (Spring 2022)

"Account for Average Wear" and "Trust," in *Phenomenal Literature: A Global Journal Devoted to Language and Literature*, Volume 7, issue 1, New Delhi, India (July-Sept. 2022)

"Short-Sighted Super" and "Hope for the Season," in *Blue Collar Review, Journal of Progressive Working Class Literature*, Volume 26, Issue 1, Norfolk, VA (Fall 2022)

"Shared Experience" [original version] and "Private Composition" in *Blackbox Manifold*, University of Cambridge, Cambridgeshire, Issue 29, UK/University of Sheffield, Sheffield, South Yorkshire, UK (January 2023)

"Thin Tally," "In Trust," "Integration," "Fabric to Mend," and "Sharp Eye," in *Literary Yard*, Great Noida West, National Capital Region, Uttar Pradesh, India (February 3rd, 2023)

"Low Matter" and "Already Worked Out," in *The Journal*, #68, Bridgend, Mid Glamorgan, Wales, UK, (February 2023)

"Capacities" and "Short Break," in *Writer's Block*, University of Amsterdam, Amsterdam, The Netherlands (February 2023)

"Score," in *Lone Stars Magazine*, #101, San Antonio, TX (February 2023)

"Fluid Situation" and "Gentle Reminder" in *Down in the Dirt*, Vol. 205, "My Homeland," Scars Publications, Gurney, IL (March 2023)

"Agreeable Empyrean," "Exceptional Moment," "Fugitive Relief," and "Projector," in *Lothlorien Poetry Journal* (March 13th, 2023)

"Peeve," in *Fast Pop* blog, Detroit, MI (June 2023)

"Blocks," "Tour," and "Turnover," in *New Pop Lit*, Detroit, MI (May 2023)

"Blues Cast" and "Spun Gold," in *Westview: A Journal of Western Oklahoma*, Volume 37, Issue 1, Southwestern Oklahoma State University, Weatherford, OK (Spring 2023)

"Progressive Infusion," "Grounded," and "A Portion of Success," in *Poets' Espresso Review*, Volume 14, Issue 5 (August 2023)

"Strike," in *Jasper's Folly Poetry Journal*, issue #2 (September 2023)

"Final Significance," in *Beatnik Cowboy* (September 20th, 2023)

"Telling Take," "Animal Instincts," and "Work Related," in *Transom*, Issue 17 (September 2023)

"No Bother" [revised version], in *Orbis: Quarterly International Literary Journal*, #205, West Kirby, Wirral, Cheshire, UK (Autumn 2023)

"Firm Realization," "Charge Into," and "Possible Improvement," in *Lost Lake Folk Opera*, V. 8, n. 1, "Waterways" Issue, Autumn 2023, Rushford, MN (Autumn 2023)

"Spot Assessment" [revised version], in *Borderless*, October 2023 (October 16th, 2023)

"Framed Declaration," in *The Bluebird Word: An Online Literary Journal for Poetry and Flash*, October 2023 issue, (October 22nd, 2023)

"Held Over," "Capable Span," and "Squamous Serenity," in *Synkroniciti*, November 30th Issue: Vol. 5, No. 4, "Space" (November 2023)

"Simple Symposium," in *Panoplyzine*, Issue 25 (September 2023)

"Reestablishment" and "Pharos," in *Active Muse: A Journal of Literature, Poetry, and Art*, Pune, India, and Boston, MA (Shishir [Winter] Issue, December 26th, 2023)

"Uncertain License," in *Evening Street Review*, Number 40, Sacramento, CA (Winter, 2023)

"Nary a Thought" and "Logical Application" in *Does It Have Pockets*? (January 1st, 2024)

"Refreshing Verisimilitude," "Transaction," "Critical Eye," "Inundation," and "Conjurers," *Lothlorien Poetry Journal* (March 16th, 2024)

"The Inalienable" and "B.Y.O. Exclusion," in *DarkWinter Literary Magazine*, Ontario, CAN (April 4th, 2024)

"Wanderlust," "Rival Faith," and "Current Vacuum," in *The Gorko Gazette* (April 26th, 2024)

"Sea Wrack," in *Down in the Dirt*, Volume 219, Gurnee, IL (May 2024)

"Dear Psyche," in *Poetry Salzburg Review*, No. 41, Salzburg, AUT (Summer 2024)

"Potential Conflagration," "Pension," "Facial Recognition," and "Caution Close," in *New Pop Lit*, Detroit, MI (Summer 2024)

"Stopgap," in *Mudfish 24*, Brooklyn, New York, NY (July 2024)

"Service, No Shoes," in *Poetry Superhighway* (July 29th, 2024)

"Goods and Services" [revised version], *Caveat Lector*, Summer 2024 Issue, San Francisco, CA (August, 2024)

"Egalitarian Outcome," in *The Field Guide Poetry Magazine* (September 28th, 2024)

"Charged Atmosphere," in *The Main Street Rag*, Volume 29, Number 4, Charlotte, NC (Fall 2024)

"At Liberty" and "Noted," in *Poets' Espresso Review*, Volume 14, Issue 6, Stockton, CA (Autumn 2024)

"Casual Glance" and "Divergence," in *Active Muse: A Journal of literature, poetry, and art*, Pune, #55 Shirshir (2024), Maharashtra, IND, and Quincy, MA, USA (December 11th, 2024)

"Total Recall" and "In Perpetuity," in *Abbey*, #177, Columbia, MD (December 2024)

"Leeway," in *Caveat Lector*, Vol. 35, no. 1, San Francisco, CA (January 14th, 2025)

"Proper Maintenance," in *The Gorko Gazette* (January 16th, 2025)

"Heated Overstatement," in *Down in the Dirt*, Gurnee, IL, Volume 228, "Murder by Burger" (February 2025)

"Deep Challenge," "Former Integrity," "Open Letter," "Safe Inside," and "Transferable Skill," in *Literary Yard*, Great Noida West, National Capital Region, Uttar Pradesh, India (February 14th, 2025)

# Observations:

### Elevation

My favorite public garbage can
sits here near the corner, often
in shade but always convenient

on my hungry way that needs
a stop for water, banana, and depot
for the peel whose bulk is now

unnecessary, plus the versatile
napkin having performed its
functions. So I celebrate the hollow

on this undistinguished curb,
chipping and lacking in historical marker,
but in a perfect spot and never too shallow.

## Road and Crew

They are stripping the streets
as one might peel dead
sunburned skin from a forearm

more or less straight but they
pummel with pneumatic hammers
and pick with curved and heavy blades

that tired pavement so turn it
into cookie crumbles that crunch
under my slow tires directed by fluorescent

flags, arrowed lights, and reddened arms
that will peel with tattoo ink or not, no shield
from the sun that August imposes, gouging

into tissue with unseen axes and pikes that will
expose the injury and lasting legacy upon and under
hides much younger than the streets just feet below.

# Unequal Opportunity Employer

Oh, to have the skill of the window-
washer, wrists snaking, swiveling

the squeegee then "snap," the fluid
crashes to beads in the bucket,

and the plate glass reflects the truth
without any streak or smudge,

a labor of transparency if one
can coordinate instrument and arm

so left to the deft and rhythm-
minded—no need for the graceless,

leaving trails, a squeaking T under
ham-fists, fingers, to apply.

### Account for Average Wear

My weeds are worn, the warp and weft
exposed, ragged right angles off

the cuff and open lattice of thread
inviting any thorn and serrated edge

to snag and shred down to the possible
unweaving of the fabric, spinning

to air (unspun!) and a pile of tangled
hair from no head, if given enough

pulling time, as my flesh will when
that hook finds an errant bit so start

my turn to stone and bone that will
last even dry and unthinking in its doom

longer than any duds no matter
the quality of its artisan and their loom.

# Trust

Rain has drummed upon the morning
so the humidity is up, and feet
are clinging to our floor's hardwood

so take a bit more of the second
to place the sole, raise it again,
feeling the surface holding the skin

the extra time a warm comfort
to reassure one walks on solid
foundations whose boards and beams

will not collapse into the maw
or shudder as if on tropical stilts
in a hurricane wind, reaffirming

our solidity and mass that must
heed the pull of gravity mother
who whispers to us that we are

not yet air and less, light as ghosts

## Private Composition

The grit from the concrete steps
has imprinted a series of notes
upon the old straight lines

of my knee's loose skin, no bloody
dissonance, only a silent staff
upon which I may compose a soaring score

whose harmonies only I may
hear in subtle sympathy with my
flex and strain as I perform the task

and lift the weight, remove the obstacle
from this portion of the day, which
might grow to the heft and tangle

of unwelcome weed, so nip this growth
in the bud, to my working song that lightens
my load, buoys me in the salt sea

of average labor where my sweat mingles
with the minutes of maintenance—the everyday
melody of unrecorded *opera minora*.

# Thin Tally

My fingers are scored with the incisions
of these dry days, my skin shrinking,
unable to meet the square-inch
requirements of the underneath
uncaring bones, so separating
in pain and small slices,

invisible even though
shouting in their sharp zing
until well after I am aware of the results
of inadequate coverage as my cells
huddle too close for their function,

in jealousy of the water that must be shared
in generous flow for one to remain whole.

# Integration

Steam flowers from a dark stem
of the hospital that bear a sign
stating, "no emergency facilities"

so must be of some specialized ilk
of whose mysteries many will wonder
on a driving-by then roll to other thoughts

while that water vapor keeps rising to mix
with the sky's own blossoms that garland
at intervals the gray barely distinguishable

from today's layers above this main artery
at whose side reaches this efflorescence of brick
whose light inners string to the sky without

yielding its vascular secrets, yet weaving
the web with all that is open and within
notice to any who take the seconds to watch.

## Sharp Eye

The street light thought no one was looking,
but I caught it hiding its ray in an instant—

Pop!

—the light was secreted in its pocket—

until its reliable eye realizes the duty again
in the diminishing of day as it meets night

to mimic what came before even if a poor
counterfeit yet necessary nonetheless

in this civic grid and more so anxious
age to lead the way over ground and through

the air who must follow the offering
of the sun and its substitute if all are not be blind.

## Low Matter

The albedo of this orange is not
as pale as the moon or sun in haze

of late afternoon, but resists the dark
and shadow just as well as those bodies

celestial and bright, exalted in the uncontained
sky that puts my limited space to shame,

whose walls are thick and stubbed, no length
to grasp and reach, but at least can hold

the inner crescent of a citrus rind (better: zest)
whose concavity, though soft and decaying,

can in this quantum shine.

## Already Worked Out

Dreaming has exhausted me,
and I arise, cramped, with underlids
puffed as with the sand of night still

weighing the folds, full scales
with the heft of blind coin
pressed upon the lashes

that keep the sleeper closed
and dead to the world while the mind
exerts its muscle, curling my spine

to infant posture, a crustacean,
a crescent only ready to shrink
and wane while the young day waxes

to clarion calls of upright activity
and crisp locomotion, coordination,
which my tendons, ligaments, repel,

cranky rebels against the cause
that will in minutes, hours unfurl
me, whose head must clear

of oneiric mist to make a go
of these sixteen hours where
phantasms ever fear to tread.

## Short Break

For once (or maybe twice)
the pigeons please—as they
burst, on the impetus of fright's

instinct like a mess of marbles
burst by a skilled thumb and index
finger or a triangle of billiards

under the impact of a brilliant
break by a forceful stick and subtle
aim, the spheres scattering like a live

still life of a chrysanthemum
crazily in bloom—before the feathers,
fingers of flapping irregularity

ruin the pristine, perfect forms
almost Platonic that rush out to their
usual pecking, wobbling, whose presence

is now a cause, a call for some master
to re-rack, reassemble—just start a new game.

# Agreeable Empyrean

Spittle has constellated the sky
of my deep blue pillow case over the course

of my proprietary night though I
will not name these formations

whose permanence is only until
the next wash when my celestial

canvas will be clean until the next
night when seven hours will heat up

my private suns so spangle the surface
in the quiet process, a Little Un-Bang,

of building my Milky Way upon warmed
fabric so agreeable to fragile, finicky cheek

a kind universe into which I may fall unawares
into no vacuum, zero pressure, and absolute freeze.

## Exceptional Moment

The heat's lash has curled
the phone line atop the obsidian
curve of the car that idles in front
of mine. So directing the suddenly

black licorice strand back into
the shimmering blue air and some
destination of the eyes that are prey
to the illusion of the earth's fervor

under the sun, which often blinds
us to the truth and its authority
of the straight line leading to a
practical place we must follow

if taken to task—which, at times—
we may avoid if only still
and dreaming, forced by route
and circumstance to look—only—

so free to see in curves
that refuse the rein of cold right.

## Peeve

Pull that hangnail rising like a flag
flapping in a breeze of non-concern
though catching my eye like a barbed

hook replete with rankling hairs so not
letting my attention go, but racking it
with the thought of tear and blood

—the anxiety in anticipating when it will rip—
and pain the owner—who might then regret
his indolence and indifference when more

raw flesh breathes the new air in crimson
exposure as the finger-end resembles more rag
than bone I silently urged him to not leave alone.

**Turnover**

The cancer ate up the proprietress some
years ago so the neighborhood presents

a different color when I make an infrequent
return to its cozy commercial streets

wherein stands her erstwhile coffee shop
still clad in its painted brick behind which hides

a magnolia beneath which to sit in agreeable
weather to enjoy the warm brew and green

leaves under her and her husband's purview
now transferred to unknown others who

are now imposing a novel rule and regimen hued
to their choice but under the identical shade.

# Spun Gold

His mother warns the tow-headed
lad of five or six years that all four
legs of the chair must touch the floor,

but the tot favors three so pushes
and swivels on this number then crashes
to that floor of which she warned him before,

yet rises with top more of a mop
and a spring in laughter as well,
abashed a bit by the will of the seat

that wouldn't stand his brand
of sitting, thus mom admonishes—
says she told him so, but listening

now is not for his soul. He spins toward
the low window's glass, a heel or some toes
on the linoleum squares in his *pas d' un*.

May his luck wind out with his tumbling
years, beyond mom's clasping words
and this somewhat soft, semi-safe room.

## Grounded

The way lies across the fresh black
asphalt that might still hold dear

the lower gray whose scars
the steamroller has healed—

pressure and heat the curatives
for this affliction of age and use

since this route is under—as all
real roads must be—so probably

keeps the memory as inscription
to dispel the fiction that this street

is untrodden, its dark the oblivion
of the sightless pristine.

## Final Significance

Apropos for the Bantam edition
of some *Canterbury Tales* to be sitting

on top of the toilet's tank,
in Modern English translation, next to the shitting,

certainly a concern of Chaucer
for its naturalism or metaphorical potential

the paradox that noisome dross
can be gold nugget and so value exponential

to the trained eye and subtle mind
far above the level of the squatting behind

## Telling Take

This Polaroid's white border
marks the limit of the present,

separates the stuff of fast, live
color from the yellowing past

where I, in Toughskins jeans
that flare moderately at the calves,

hold the pickerel my father
has caught and try to curl

a smirk around my baby teeth
as the big fish's own insist

upon digging their close-ranked
needles into flesh of forefinger and thumb,

and its slick weight threatens to pull
down my single-digit arm,

from wrist all the thin way to the socket,
leaving me limp, unable to raise a rampart

to crane up the water-kingdom's prize
for the backyard display and awe.

*

Perhaps I should have been wearing
only Somewhat-Toughskins

(despite their reinforced fabric squares
guarding—grass-stained—growing knees).

or at least a name qualified by the scant strength
that the age of little body-hair brings

*

I think the vanquished beast would win
If I had to pose at length, frozen-proud
in imitation of paternal glory,
but the photo, slightly curling,

if taken from the ancient album
doesn't speak, but I'll reveal the secret

strain, leave the lad to tough it out
between the faux-leather covers,

more years to proffer his grit
to any rare seekers, takers

in the unquestioning—
unquestioned—hollow

of a closet's keeping,
a silent, storied dark.

# Animal Instincts

Battler, pill bug—
feelers ahead and above—
in its segmented silver
crustacean armor defies
gravity upward along
our yellow bathroom wall.

The stretched flesh
of the punch-swollen fist
defies the same,
stiff and iced—
still adrenaline-drunk
at four a.m.

well after the bars have closed
and longer since the knuckles
flew into bone,

so if the unnatural way
is natural after all, let us hope
for it all the way as our
carbon and water combos

of whatever configuration
fight the drag to downward
upon walls upon carpet or concrete
scuttle, swell, or saunter—
erect, upright.

## No Bother

The scrawl of marginalia decorating
the difficulties of the poem does not

irk me as I discover my own conundrums
and cruxes churning through dense

woods of words to phrase to stanza depth
because a second-hand text is fair game

for found ink and rough graphite lines,
shapes, circles, and twists of inscrutable

cursive or print, the publisher's own
now an accepted palimpsest on paper

rather than vellum in this age vanishing
to binary code and infinitely flickering,

infatuating screen that will preclude
this communion with an unknown precursor

leaving the last, recent reader lonely without
these relict Arabesques of accumulated perplexity

and questions semi-legible but sure evidence
of siblinghood—those seeking significance,

understanding, the scratchings and stainings
clues, crumbs of intimation for the next

## Possible Improvement

The sidewalks on Wilkins Avenue
are only paved in grass, both sides,
if one pauses to check, so soft, dark,

and dewy to the tread, a surprise
if one is looking up or straight
ahead in half-aware expectation

of concrete and its hard conversation
the tap-tap, clap-clap that would
continue at least to the curb

then hushed if stepping onto
the asphalt street and its quiet
disposition and deference to wheels

as well as the rhythm of feet that
would recover from the springy
shock determined after seconds

to be quite the comfort, pleasant
exception before the quick return
to the clackety-clack of the aggregate

gravel, lime, and water, cured
of the ground's old give, its
ancient unfinished rebound.

## Spot Assessment

These skeleton keys hail from Portugal,
states the hand-drawn phrase on gray

cardboard, which provenance unlocks
my thinking as to what is so special

about these thin fingers of old iron and brass
that to my lay-eyes do not appear any different

from the domestic variety that might sell
for far less especially as used item and even

worse lacking the complementary locks,
necessary for utility securing some equally lost

door or chest, but in which some expert
in Iberian antiques might find money

and historical value. I cannot rid

thus, my doubt of the sign's worth

and the wares, better left to the keener sight
and mind that can unlock the mystery

safe, pendant and plain before a blind view.

## Capable Span

Has the spider in the Dixie Cup rendered
said vessel unusable in the judgement of my

careful wife—as a progeny of Arachne has bridged
the gap over the diameter of accepting space

where potential for water-filling is high
and the deluge destroying the span

if she decides to avail herself of the recess
for which the factory executed the design

in the flexibility of molded paper, tight
to the drops, which, as yet, do not fall?

*

The days have run, and the critter like
an upside-down flower of filament petals

still holds tightrope center within the circle
that, dry, twangs a silent Angstrom in the room's

almost-not-there current so no solo performance
the ear might discern, but proof of the balance

the eight-legger and its silk still maintain
above insistent gravity's drag while she forbears

to disturb the hollow while I wonder if
the tiny worker keeps deft, resilient hope.

## Squamous Serenity

The road's surface is calm and quiet
at the red light, a snoozing snake's
smooth-scaled back in the day's

consistent sun that yields the calm
of warmth to those needing to bask,
which this way will not in seconds

when the cool green changes the scene
and the gray skin will be sheathed
with quicksilver that reflects the light

back up into the satiated air whose rush
now parallels the serpent waiting
for the still of space, the next stop

where the grace of soft rays will light
upon the bare plain of a brief
but repeated escape

# Reestablishment

The sun's might has faded the Turkish
restaurant's awning that once peacocked

a proud purple to the main street from its
Sublime Porte, whose empire has fallen

as all do even if merely gastronomical
rather than of geopolitical and transcontinental

expanse, so this agéd fabric must the proprietor
replace with renewed color of confidence

greeting the general public with the business'
best, if only the extent of a quarter city block,

extent curtailed by the ceding of its banquet
province to the realpolitik of sale and cash,

no more does it span the intersection, but no reason
to relinquish the heartland and let its shading

sail bleach to salt desert's gray and exhausted
white, instead raise another standard in blazing

contrast to the cool shadow for customers' comfort
as they found a new nation, a culinary republic in savory fight

## Pharos

The old poinsettia casts a shadow
upon the placemat, near the end of its
term as a signal through the dun and gray

of winter and the cancer diagnosis and succeeding
chemo that has gone better than expected
so has exceeded hope, which the scarlet

of its leaves has bannered, so we have deemed
to interpret the durable blaze of two seasons
pushing to three where life will continue

for one of the two, probably she with legs
instead of roots that gripped the soil and year
to anchor the heralding of said hope, the red

rising above the worry and fatigue, above
the months of doubt and molecular medication,
leaving them low and pliant, so far, to the hairless

one's will, the wish, to be left behind even as we
desire this flower, remnant, survivor since December
to move into the summer, the future, with us alive.

## Refreshing Verisimilitude

Peels now the paint from the store wall's
mural after years of adherence to the bricks,

to the representation of the birds above our park
and neighborhood—from a bird's eye view—

now losing its sight as the red-brown erupts
under the dry flakes half-clinging like hangnails

ready to cleave from the living skin, which will,
like these early emigrants, slough off

and leave the scene to one's imagination
if no brush and talent refresh the hard surface

with colors and shapes that will place the sky
and attending feathers upon the solid, upright

angle of convenience and commerce,
with even a hint of a breeze above these trees

## Transaction

Branches, the crabbed hands
of spindly giants, crack and drop,

a windfall this winter to spring
as the tender does not, cannot survey

then circumambulate the lawn to keep
these careless limbs in line, or gathered

to snap and confine to a pile doomed
to truck transportation out of the yard's

square patch steadfast against the ravine
that drops as if to an imagined sea

where one can imagine she swims eternally,
her back now finned so no more to stoop

over the grass that must receive the gifts
of the rambunctious, rattling trees

and her arms, hands, now just to push
the deep cool currents of the other ocean

while in our air the sign for sale has disappeared
like an uprooted trunk after felling of the bole

replaced by a new woman bending
to the old task with new gloves

while the fringe of her domain pushes
up snow drops in the infant spring

even as last year's largesse deigns, continues
to drop, command the heir to continue

the chore, eternal crunch

## Inundation

The long shadow of the late afternoon sun's
oil seeps, a languorous river running

to gourmand's delight in its savoring,
swallowing of the listing day's light

that has lasted long enough for the grass
and stones, a thorough deluge to drink

in eight-plus hours its own generous
and exclusive span at the board

so time to yield to the flood now
lengthening limbs of tree and walkers

to low-giant stride and shadow whose
legs stretching curb to curb will dissolve

in the solution of sunset that heralds the rising
of the sea whose depth will drown eventually

any remaining islands, igneous and rebellious,
tenacious of their last reflected glory

they must relinquish, so sink, until the uplift,
the shine, in the near star's next day

# The Inalienable

No light lurks in this half-moon
of hill, so safe from the seekings

of any eye keen to expose soft
mystery for its private profit—

best to keep swathes of secrecy
so—no need to denude the sleeping

under the sable, deft default
at this hour-arc on the globe,

security in the hidden-kept
lost under so much ill-umination,

for found is at times a taken
from the unseen with right to keep.

## Current Vacuum

For our benefit the fluorescent tube, sleek
and svelte, has deigned to hum and blink
for our benefit, who all need a show in our week

so let the alternation elude the employing powers
the seconds of illumination then less
provide variety in these working hours

that often pass in a bland and uni-tone glare
sinking spirit whose instrument is so much the eye
so enjoy the obsolescence, a job perk, a festive flair

## Sea Wrack

The black Pontiac Thunderbird sits low on the side street,
humbled to the century-old brick as the tires sit
*sans* air on the rims that have not revolved

around their axles in witnessed years
that fade the shadow to dull gray even brown
and plunge sharp teeth to vinyl roof that is now

ragged under windfall, dry leaves
crabbed like stiff bones of the hand,
and branches crooked and cured, fine for firewood

or mimics of crossed tibia on a Jolly Roger
waiting for a smiling skull just above,
pennant of a pirate who might not deign

to seize this still hunk with ancient
automatic shift on the steering column
over plush faded red velvet bench seats

as choice booty for captain's share
and a crew's division as well, so leave
it, as the owner has done, thus relinquishing

the deed to the city seas on which this Detroit
detritus is slowly sinking under gravity's weight
and the patient crustaceans, carapaces of subtle rust

# Dear Psyche

How feels the concrete of the sidewalk
through the eating man's jeans?

Does the bun and ground beef of survival
suffice for evaporated pride that must be

hanging, *farfalla*-persistent about six
feet in the near air, strollers-by, storefront

height, where the glass of this level might
even reflect the faint soul taken as most

as a glare of sun-chicanery under mid-day
rays, but which follow him when he rises

from the low meal and rejoins his peers
on the straight-legged terrace, a stand-up above?

# Pension

A rolling stone gathers no moss goes the saw
so a sitting tire on its aging air certainly will grow

green as I have seen, as if a black stone standing
on end under the rusting frame of a van that the seventies

of the previous century spawned, now showing its age
and inability to attract anymore some happenin' chicks

so sitting out of memory in some obscure, untended alley
under scrawny sumac shade on a crammed, cindery

lot whose privacy is usually sealed, assured except
for the curious eye in rare chance passing that notes

the emerald sheen which has colonized the rubber long
since still, a companion in retirement, quiet, even

content to dream with the surely drained battery
and the spent hulk of bitchin' rides and making the scene

## Goods and Services

As we pass, your glare penetrates
the lenses of your glasses to slash

at me for the flashing instant
as our eyes shift briefly to meet,

which conference yields to blind
sidewalks above which I hear strained sobs

rising from your throat then diminishing
in our own discrete distances that will

negate the knowledge of each other
and the possibility of succor I might

offer you even in return
for the sharpened blades you have

thrown me no matter how blunt
and ready to offer flowers

of solace that would bloom despite
the waste between us.

**Noted**

Flits the so less appreciated moth through
the somnolent air approaching a dim midnight

wings old-newspaper fit only for wrapping fish
let alone drawing any eyes of appreciation

as slumber creeps, a rising tide, high
in a few hours, so efforts aimed must be

conserved for fliers of note, sun-stroking
butterflies full of orange gems or blue

fluttering upon the bright air of many hours ago,
so this endeavor in black upon white in those

very hours though lacking nectar or flowers must mark
the interest stoked by that night-one of brown and gray

## Casual Glance

An ex's Facebook photo shows a glass
of red wine in her hand at the end

of a phoenix-tatted arm, a deep symbol,
she explains on the virtual page,

of a rebirth from loss, whose raw edge
*vino rosso* may help dull.


As I recall, she always did like her reds and whites,
so I helped her on occasion finish a bottle,

those nights a few decades gone
when we were together within spring and summer.


Now I manage a glass—or, rarely—two a week
with savory dinners, wiser, I suppose, with accumulated years

that have squeezed out the grapes
to leave unadulterated water flowing

through my veins to wet the flowers
my wife has nurtured in our seasons

that return and return—which my brief
three months with the other never will.

## Total Recall

I cannot torque my neck so must remain curious
of the walker upon the passing sidewalk,

hair of (I think) pink, so as not to be injurious
to my neck, shoulders, and fellow flowing cars

so must consign the sight to memory, which is often spurious,
as distance and desire distort what was once truth

thus rob the real of a departed day, to render it penurious
while upgrading the uncertain image to what must have been

## Proper Maintenance

Before the aged toenail cuts to semi-freedom
from black depth of sock, snip that very offender

after no more than thirty days, a preemptive
slice against the keratin that would poke

from within, marring the black or gray
of my lowest fabric with a spot of flesh

a pale signal that it's closing time
for this length of vestigial tree-climber tool

presumptuous in straining for the sun
beyond the curved leather though perhaps

only akin to the prime mover above, atop
the bones against whose stones we wish

to rise up, above

## Safe Inside

The pain is moderate—just a stubbing
of the little toe—which I contain as if boxing

a sharp blade after cushioning it in paper
to double the dulling during the transport

of the continuing day where I must dwell
with exposed legs, feet, and digits, continually

moving between obstacles that sometimes
may meet such pioneers, with hope that I can

continue to gift-wrap such nerve-wracks,
keep safe and managed until the pain

drains to memory instead of being swallowed
by a monster, a wave thrice my size

no wrapping can anesthetize, just give
free throbbing reign that engulfs all the outside

# Recollections:

**Equipoise**

Mundy Street dips and rises
where the old mines hollowed

out its legs, so one day might
collapse as a man well drunk

or fighter struck with a Joe Frazier
left hook. So must have been more

stable when the beverage outlet
sat on a level lot back from this

bending, breaking asphalt where
dad garnered his twelve bottles

of beer in a latticed wooden case
and we were left with the choice

of soda flavors an equal twelve—
so a welcome stop even if off-brands—

but always a few colas and lemon-limes
to eight of miscellany—root beer,

glowing orange, or even sometimes cream—
variety enough in the ratio and wisdom

of the double choices to take back
up the mountain beyond the roller-coaster

of this road in the East End, sweet for us
and sedating for him again on solid ground.

## The Trend Set

Summer 1985 flowered forth a slump-
shouldered dude in jacket and slacks of mint green

with peach T-shirt that must have
matched, thus demonstrated Don Johnson

and Philip Michael Thomas as Crockett
and Tubbs—so emulated by this plumber

on a Sunday night at the pony track
fourteen-hundred miles north of Miami

and its vice, with his snaggled, gray-yellow
teeth clamping the swizzle-straw

between explanations of his sartorial choice
to us, who drank—underage—

thanks to our friend behind the bar—like adults—

just like the man in his
subtropical fibers

dressing up to play the role
of hip hero in ill-fitting duds

until draining the drinks to their watery dregs.

## Short-Sighted Super

She referred to me as the bald guy
to my colleague temp but, though
true to a considerable degree, I felt
the epithet did not take into account

my other qualities that, though not
Homeric, were worthy to rise
as the cream of my character to some
effervescent appellation such as

Trusted Short-Term Employee
or Always Arrived by Eight A.M.
despite the scant visual imagery
attached to these honorable monikers,

in response to which I would certainly
raise my shining pate whose Pharos-like
function would be eclipsed by the light
of my merits understood but unseen

## Shared Experience

The diver's arc launched him down
into blue-gray depths that would
wait out eternity for the splash
of his brown-red body that now
pended in stone-white air, uncaring

of the longest wait between the ashlar
leap and sparse tree curving above
the patient pool, all in ancient
Paestum while I watched, having
landed in a comfortable chair

in front of the painted slab that once
was the underside of a ponderous
lid separating the quick from the dead
before the excavation and museum role,
whose setting I was now enjoying

but could only linger minutes for
the sea-seeker to find the deep
untouched for twenty-five centuries,
so gazed with calm and concentration
through the scant cloth of time

that fell to my lot by Campanian bones
thrown by gods of *Mare Nostrum* who
wouldn't understand the painter's tongue
but might the pigment upon the piece
of cut rock that we both considered

despite the difference between my small
plot on the earth and their dominions
of sky and ocean, whose tiny imitation
lay open for me who would soon
depart upon his own determined arc.

## Capacities

Now I see you wear a black
belt around your torso,
which features two handles.

Have you become cargo—
professor—to be loaded
and packed off to a pre-determined

destination of post-stroke,
certainly not your choice?

So perhaps I can forgive you
for the hand on the small
of my back during office

afternoons in the independent
study of a language defunct
and disabled—and the surprise

kiss on my cheek after translation
with dual-tongue text,
verso and faithful recto

providing aid unnecessarily
with your learning present
and ready answer of enthusiasm.

Your body you now call "a wreck"
as I grasp the handles and pull
you up would still obey

your *mandatum* if it could,
to tutor and teach but now totters
until it stills under my arm's

control, and my sense that only
directs me to steady your ruined
gate that might remember its past impress.

# Score

I ripped the outer edge of my elbow
as I lunged at his little brother threatening
to throw the football into the forest,

slipping on the cesspool-slick weeds
that made up the majority of the lawn
behind the small subsidized home,

leaving a flap of seventh-grade skin
to heal into a scar like a smooth smile
or frown that bends hairless to this day

if one happens to notice this obscure
corner of my fleshly self, which is free
of shackles unlike that brother who,

I have been told, is behind bars
for the long term and a crime unknown
to me that must be worse than trying

to take the ball and end the game on account
of some small cause and subsequent pique
that will never be recorded in the final score

## Fluid Situation

Whiskey sways you at the top
of the stairs so my embrace
will save you from a harsh descent
and allow the shepherding of you
into the bedroom for the best
of your full and open body topped
by the Kentucky bourbon of your
kissing breath that further pricks
my callow lust on this prom night
on which to make many possible
mistakes if one is too eager to care
among the overpowering heat
of new pleasure among spaces
forbidden but free now to the will
of innocence desiring its melting end

# Gentle Reminder

Not very beachy on this city beach backed
by a wall of somewhat crumbling concrete
scrawled with old and incomplete graffiti

and the graying asphalt basketball courts
close upon the cigaretted sand whose
substance must be in sync with the dead

and scattered ash, a mélange sticking
to the boots' bottoms, lugs lugging the bits
back to the base within their rubber teeth

as sharp as those of the sharks that do not
swim in this inland sea anyway,
a competition of one against none so

losing grains gradually without a concern
for the loss of first place and private acclaim,
which will continue as long as these steps

stride upon the city and its gritty edges
at the lake's limen with its respectful waves
reminding any paying attention that the water

still laps and rolls stones to polished marbles
and beads that murmur in the greeting of surf
still pushing up its track and back though not

public transportation in steel and fluorescence
yet transport enough

## Projector

Driven to drive-in movies as children, clad
in our pajamas, so sensed by parents
the transition from waking
to not, the ninety minutes

upon the screen whose size obscured
the evening and night so ushered
in the descent while still in the backseat,
unbelted, into deep dream for one tot

or more who had had enough of the day
long since dark, and now lay, limp,
upon home-return, within the care-folds
of adult arms against the heavy drop

to the earth of that day given farewell
by the G-rated film, second feature
on the double-bill unnecessary
to shuffle the seven-year-old

and siblings less off to eyes
opening no earlier than the next
morning whose face would rise
without interruption and star only the sun

## Blues Cast

Just an overnighter
at the city jail,
drunken and disorderly
at a fern bar
(when those were the rage)

accompanying the wee hours
with renditions of blues tunes
by artists certainly more skilled
than these two

but useful for their situation
against the bars and their steel
rhythm through the span
to sobering that led concurrently

to a dawn as white as an etiolated
stalk under a dull-heavy rock

not to Mississippi and Miss Liza,
just a drain of irregular income,
a hangover-headsplitter, and eternal
banishment from the faux-fiddlehead

garden of Eden, arch-officer Michael or not,
no flaming sword, just a cool baton at the door.

# Progressive Infusion

The cold tea at the trending
restaurant in the Embarcadero
was of chrysanthemum and its intrigue,

and, in little time, the waiter
deposited a glass apropos
for *vin blanc* in whose liquid

floated a single, shaggy golden flower
whose effect of old cigarettes
the patron now imbibed, noted

the flat, dust encumbrance
of ash tray on the tongue
now part of the meal, and addition

to the appetizer, appealing as the price
and barn-wood of the tables, whose grain
and lacquer, at least, they would not taste.

## A Portion of Success

I chose the wrong trail
while ascending Angel Island

so missed the summit in my
parsed-out time though I did

glimpse the top where those
eponyms take flight or alight

whom a pilgrim might see
if in the correct loft of mind

even upon a false path, a fire
lane, only circling the crown

like a tonsure in reverse,
the eucalyptus massing

dark and dream-thick on each
side to confound the climber

on a sweating quest to the apex
commanding the attendant bay,

where near-heaven meets earth
at a sharp final edge, a port

for destinations down and up
whose node will bestow

a blessing even upon the hoofer,
head befuddled and point unachieved.

## Strike

Wedge-driving requires the sharp
edge perpendicular to the rings
for no age of the fallen tree

is the concern of the steel's bit
submerging into fiber's sea
until reaching the bottom,

so clanking upon soil or stone
beneath and taken up again
to sink sharp tooth and pounds

into another depth whose thick
waters will provide heat
under the strike of flame

but only after these hefty strokes
of the sledgehammer flush upon the blunt
and mushrooming—little rusted—head

that will ring into the abyss, a beacon
sounding the drop, drop, drop of the progress
hoped true for the crisp split

of one into two or four, manageable
morsels for the closed stove of cast
iron to digest in its infernal belly

much hotter than the body with its sweat
and hands aching from the impact
of handle and metal to metal,

remembering the needed blows
in muscles and connecting tissue,
mindful for several days of crackle

and combustion 'til another week
to descend upon the surface
of the sectioned oak and drive,

drive, drive that sharp end
through the standing sentinels
until the cylinders halved, quartered
convenient for a stack against
the wall's bricks and a bundle
in the arms' compass to carry

into the needing home where
the mercury is lowering
but the heavy wood, tricked

by muscle, forge, and brother
branch is now compliant,
perfect now for springing alight.

## Work Related

Thunk!—the usual—no . . .

a sliver of sharp sound
through the cardboard's corrugated hide

the beast is broken

a tang sweet and medicine bitter,

shadow spreading outward, under the box

dampens the concrete and steel lip
underbiting at the open truck-dock

> "Damn—I think we finally broke a bottle,"
> says one of the bending team to the other
>
> within the close confines of the trailer
> as the aroma wafts—"peach or something"—

But they can only resume removing the cartons
from the deposited palette, push the leaker to the side,
await the boss's response, hope he lets slide

the honest mistake in the heat of effort—
one of a thousand spirits if not more—

imagine the orchard while the fumes rise
in the still summer afternoon,

just beyond the bleached asphalt,

waiting with sweet fruit and cool juice.

### Firm Realization

On the yellow brick—alley—I bottomed out
and am certain my undercarriage bears

the scars—an ignorant hope of short cut—
turned my wheels right, onto the hump—

and—bump!—bump! I rued my choice
in the battering instant but moved forward

still until the baked clay leveled and I
left it for soft asphalt of the frequented street

with hope (the second in seconds)
in the soundness of my steel for future

integrity and use, no leaking fluid,
debility, plus the delay and *dinero*

of repair, which, so far, has been fulfilled,
and roll with the stony punches months

since delivered, cognizant of shifting surfaces
and the hard fist of upcurving earth meeting me below

# Held Over

Terracina carves a gentle crescent below
the high hill where the low remains of the temple

of Jupiter Anxur stand near the old Appian Way
overlooking the sea just south

of *Il Capo Circeo* shielding the sight
from the shores that lead to Rome, whose

arches and consequent cryptoporticus
furnish enough cool empty space

under the Tyrrhenian sun, no need for descent
into old or new town or cutting edge of *la spiaggia*

or further passage north into Lazio's heart
beyond this view of the shimmering moon

outspread below, so much brighter than
its far twin celestial, so much above this—

but shy at this sustained moment of high
Mediterranean azure sky but—no worry—

no need now for the silver sheen and bewitching
beams, under these ancient curves that no

longer support a cella for the discarded god,
the supercession clear and the vacant

space in which imagination may raise
architectural orders, marble walls, and shelter roof,

satis—as this bay and height for this hour—
an arc of *abbastanza*, the welcome umbra

of a long hour's cerulean stay,
a blessed midday bower

## Uncertain License

First day of trout fishing, and my
dad was still on the banks of the stream,

so grandpa drove me home, a mis-
understanding, to our house empty

of mother or other to supervise me,
at six, so I kept the doors locked

and kept to the kitchen, not fear
exactly but just never before

on my own in any abode, the shock
of the new as I looked at the trees

from the window in early bud,
an innocent green to grow deep

in the season's course, just taking
a while to overcome the chill and wind

safe, at least, from the blades of winter,
soon summer would shed the tattered

memory of a tenuous time, a cool stretch,
and seven would come warm to me.

## Nary a Thought

"She's a little downbeat,
a little too much into

'What does this poem
say about death?'—

you know what I mean?"

    Since I wanted the year-long
    position, I replied that

"I didn't even think about death
until I was twenty-seven,"

which was my previous year
so leaving this one open

for the thought that really had been
rustling about for a decade or even

longer like a stealthy animal
in a crawl space,

but that beast remained silent,
away from administrative ears,

and we left the subject with easy
smiles like the ones

that would spread on faces
after pleasant reads

in the fall across from summer's
lazy gap when some other

teacher took the hint
and temporary substitution.

## Logical Application

"You can have the shotgun
or the dogs," proclaimed the future
suicide to us pre-teens as we sailed

the portion of creek that strayed
through his land—after my mate
responded to his initial command

to vacate: "You don't own the water
in the creek"—fluid logic for ten
years or so upon this thinking earth,

of which, a tiny portion belonged
to this man who would, in a generation
lose all hope and relinquish

his rights to property he was now
asserting with the threat of buckshot
and fang to be applied to insolent

interlopers and one's flowing casuistry,
floating along with inner tube and plastic
tub upon that cool public liquid

they would relinquish upon utterance
of the unpleasant choices, one of which,
upon an interminable diagnosis, in the cold

stream of years, he would visit upon his destined self.

# Conjurers

I'm certain the cat was watching us
every time we passed its human's
bungalow in the fifty-five and up park

in sunny Florida where the humid breeze
was slinking off the Intracoastal Waterway
with its not-even-whispered clues of the near

tropic flora not as secret as that set of whiskers
and furry pointed ears that must be present
under frond or front step in our revolutions

that could not spin fate in our favor or whisk
away the knowledge of mother lying her last
in the ICU and our lack of power to reverse

the course that another force, unstoppable,
had sent her on almost a week ago
while we were up in the temperate zone

too far and unaware to intervene, so now
we circumambulate, satellites without a sun,
in hopeless hope for a magic circle, twined

and twined, which Mr. Boots and his whiskers
witnesses, sympathy signaled in his sharp eyes
that catch us, futile, and the dying light.

## B.Y.O. Exclusion

She brought her own beer to the dinner
party and soon directed her

conversation to the known couple
arranged at an angle to the other pair

at the table, which, square, should
have been miles long, and a rectangle

receding into range of non-existence,
so she could quaff her private brew

in the company of the favored two

like a prized vintage among the swill,
with whom she wanted her guts to spill.

## Wanderlust

Upon purchase of a used copy of Salinger's
*Nine Stories* and a quick glance at his
oeuvre on a blank front page, I began
to question if I had read *Franny and Zooey*
During some pre-millennial year so must,

I believe, have purchased said mystery text,
right? As I, the hero of this narrative,
write, create, more than only peruse
so certain of my engagement, unlike
with that novel of the famous recluse,

when living up in New Hampshire
near the river's divide with Vermont,
still sought by pilgrims, worshippers,
only the rare fortunate admitted
into the celebrated presence, long august,

so now another reader may not wonder
why I cannot remember if I read the work
in question since my interpolation of northern
New England, no, my own peregrinations
display my tendency of just going on—and off

## Rival Faith

For the greater portion of the seven-day
span down at the shore, I determined to stay

salt-clean so kept away from the fresh-water
warm shower in the rental, proclaiming

the purity of mother ocean's several
times daily cleanse so superior at least

for the duration of bathing trunks and flip-flops
in the middle of July, my brined self

a continual lustration to those marine gods
who would, in return, keep me fresh

and redolent of a tidal line's tang, warding
off any odor of landward sweat and attendant

earth's dirt that might have been ground
into my pickled flesh turning to sleek scale

serving me well as I slipped into form
of fish that my housemates of the week did

not appreciate, so at last netted me back to our
bathroom and it's flowered plastic curtain

behind which rained their idea of ablution
with its terry cloth, shampoo, and soap

that these fishers of supposedly unwashed
men worshipped as the only vanquisher of evil

grit and taint, thus proselytizing successfully
me, the pagan in the foam and surf,

who took sudsy baptism under the tongues
of hot municipal water, reborn to the fragrance

of fresh, deodorized for the clambakes,
corn on the cob of the final three days.

## Potential Conflagration

At the base of the ridge that undulated
like a snake, the party was happening—

twenty guys and a keg of beer near where
the land ran down to the unseen creek,

an undercurrent not unlike the threat
running through the imbibers attempting

to revel though split between two packs,
a blaze bound to ignite if spark struck and lit

since either was little known to the other

—and no welcome relief of women in sight—

so dry tinder on a hot summer evening
that was sinking almost silently into a night

that suggested a fire storm flaming up,
whose coming flames, a few attendees,

climbing back up to the level road and out,
were happy to leave in the simmer down there.

## Facial Recognition

All of that generation in the area
know the history of his disfigured

face so much that the familiarity
erases the scars and reconstructed

flesh and replaces them with the features
previous to the shotgun's blast

with its little brutes of buckshot
pocking the teen visage with leaded

holes far deeper than acne with its red
of inflammation and greasy pressure

pain, paling to the permanent marking
of close-range spray that invited

an extended convalescence and hospital
stay, finished long ago and healed, pain

evaporated so far back, old news so no
news, just the way of things for those

in time with the true tale, numbed these
days into forgotten and who cares

## Caution Close

"Dougherty, don't worry about Domanski—
you've got him beat by forty pounds"

but the former insisted on expressing his fear
and twisting his neck at all those sounds

that signaled only a leaf dropping to the walk,
but danger is a crop that best abounds

when one is unaware of common clues
so goes about oblivious to every care

but Dougherty was keen to every threat
and not—so avoided black eyes with that stare

pinned upon the appearance of that perceived beast
who never arrived—unlike his constant despair

## Stopgap

Her scattered teeth listed like tombstones
in an old graveyard, caretaker long deceased,

as her mouth opened to beg for gas money
that would take her to a new factory job

on the North Side in her car whose right
rear tire was just the temporary doughnut

spare so limiting her speed until she could
find another sum for the permanent fix

that would not bring back her friend's
daughter from Fentanyl's deadly deep

as she related while pulling out
of the supermarket's lucky lot

where a happened-upon listener delivered
an Alex Hamilton honestly into her hands

beneath her weeping eyes so giving her
fuel for another chance of living in these days.

### Service, No Shoes

Second cousin Tina's boyfriend at the time
was tall enough to unscrew the spent bulb
and twist into light another—in bare feet

below his chestnut mane reaching down
as he reached up with easy arms
to the socket unattainable to mother and me

in my short age that might let me gaze
at the summit in wonder while the hands
extended breezily to the top of my bedroom's

delimited space thence to drop with a slap
upon the jeans that belled at their bottom
to leave air for the naked, confident toes

that would not stride again upon our hardwoods,
thus lucky was I that the new filament
lasted until I was enough to reach

through ingenuity or rising inches
the zenith of my realm while feet returned
in due course and the return of fashion

to shoes—and hair to collar length—
proper confines in public, I suppose,
but unnecessary integument for any kind act

# Egalitarian Outcome

I taught a descendant
of one of the myriad
ramifications o'er the sea
of the tangled Habsburg tree

that had somehow reached
the sun of this New World school,
so now strutted my destined hour
to impress my academic power

upon this callow heir
of old Iberia and Austria
who must be willing thrall
to my high position, my windfall,

whose sires luxuriating in *Die Hofburg*
or *Palacio Real* had once ignored
mine in sovereignty supercilious,
beneath even a meager glance bilious

but years one hundred and more
since Gavrilo's Balkan shot
must have dulled the hard division
and produced this ease of elision

that we enjoyed as pupil
and teacher despite my need
to bestow an honest, accepted grade
that the slumbering hierarchy, betrayed.

## Charged Atmosphere

"I've been called a walking heart attack,"
says the man, invisible, behind me on the deck,

and I wonder if he is speaking nearly literally
or just expressing his status within his circle

as a man of excitement and constant surprise
whose presence is a jolt, a jab, liable

to stop the circuits, the blood of boon companions
in a frozen twist of suspense then stunned

revelation (almost) too much for the flesh
and attending mind to take, to continue

on its average course, which cannot contend
with lightning, a god's dollop of electrical charge—

of if he if just ailing and of poor diet,
a quiet schedule leading to an early end

## At Liberty

Knowing the bay's breeze would blow away
my floppy hat, I bought a brim in the Tenderloin,

wide but anchored by a cord that I could tighten
against my neck, a confinement

for the semi-stiff fabric that orbited my skull
like a ring around Saturn, so far

from these waters and this rock whose Spanish name,
I was wonder, was known to the Birdman

or just another bar among the many from which none
escaped save Frank Morris and his vanished crew?

Whose bones were probably rolling
beneath us since no strings attached had they now

in the half-century-plus since they grew fins
and fish-stroked away into the unforgiving

salt flood to dissolve as we and my lid did my not
on that windy day even with our freedom

to tour the defunct jail shackled in infamy,
and be taken back to safe ground, hat still held tightly

on my head, the cost of coming and going
over an ocean's open arm

## Divergence

We cannot meet again, forty years
after the touch and passion, as your flesh

has joined with another to produce
new—alien from any factor of me

in the hot equation, so leaving me cold,
compounded upon the double score

that has sundered us following the initial
flash in front, back seat, and occasionally bed

when we could acquire one as illicit
adolescents looking to lie up as adults

that we now are—having overcome
the thrill and left now with the ice

of retrospect that might thaw a rivulet
at least of running wonder what if

limbs and hearts had grown intertwined
like oh so close seeds and roots

under tallying seasons of different skies

# Leeway

We were only turning around in his
driveway even if in high spirits borne
by nineteen years, but the homeowner's

silhouette against a single glaring
porch light extended from his right hand
to a monstrous digit pending nearly

to the knee, which we determined
in an adrenaline jolt, stretched
not as warm flesh darkened but cold

tense metal daring to be turned
toward our youth and discharged
in our callow direction, stop us in our

errant tracks upon the driveway's gravel
and dirt, innocent of avarice and any ill
intent, but incorrect nevertheless,

saved by the gear of quick reverse,
obedient to the anxious hand
that might have slicked the shift

with sweat even in the dark night's cool
that could not hide the error in our route
from the man in the woods, triggered resolute.

## Heated Overstatement

I don't know why I said to nobody that I wanted
to die, on that dark slushy street of a January
in Chicago where the rain only intermittently

froze to snow, needling my tired eyes
at three a.m. outside the bars open
and flowing for another wee hour

while I walked home to the reliable rhythm
of red lights and green, safe accompaniment
on the straight way back toward the lake,

a square deal on foot or even in car,
the comfort of right angles I wasn't feeling
so must have been primed to exaggerate

in my paces toward the east where the sun
would return in five hours give or take
the sluggish, winking winter minutes,

which knowledge I must have kept up
my sleeve buried under the thick aegis
of warm wool waiting for an unconscious need.

# Deep Challenge

The steep terrain was the attraction to me
at five or six when on a fishing trip to the near north
and the river whose bank here, from the quiet
road, dropped with such an angle under the trees
and tough vines by whose tenacious magic I imagined

ascending if the descent to the exposed shore
lost its luster—which was unlikely—since gravity
held such a pull on ankles anxious to challenge
the so-sloping ground unknown at home,
such a novelty in the strength drawing down

to the slack current and its lace of cobbles
then only a depth of splashing inches to its beads—
the islands, flat and fish bone-festooned—
bleaching in the sun now high and triumphant
after the declivity since conquered that would,

however, remain for the struggle back up
and the feeling of the earth's deep hand clamping
on legs so keen and happy to resist that invisible
grip that must rise up only from this naturally muscled
and enchanted spot in the world otherwise plain.

## Transferable Skill

Why learn to strike the number keys
without looking when already decided

to leave the city, so waste the working day
—as if a salaried daytime worker—

plus the subway fare—even looking
like those fortunate and eating in common

on May's sun-struck plaza so acting the part
of one who has it modestly made?


But if no one notices the difference,
the impersonation, harm is naught

since the instruction is free, and after two weeks,
one can leap, blind, over the top letter line

then carry in secret the skill five hundred miles
to the new, having gaining the ability

to punch (if needed, in the dark), the indispensable
Indo-Arabic row, marketable for the remainder of life

# Ruminations:

## Hope for the Season

The cold air will weigh down
the bullets that might fly
on these streets that have seen
their wings in nights of heat

that passed months ago
having seen their light, hot lead
alighting into present flesh,
scarce now in these lean

months whose ice, we hope,
will ride upon those hard, fast
bits, encasing them like glass,
just a harmless display that will

sink to the cracked and buckled sidewalk,
roll like a quaint child's bright marble
in one of the mothering concrete seams,
with just a sigh, no shatter or screams.

## In Trust

We cede the sense of self to parents
for our low years are blind—for others
to witness and take as their own

since we have no need of the remembrance,
which is just a phantom beyond the flesh
and its growing needs that demand and proceed

without a thought or memory spun for later
recall—which will arrive in time we won't
mark as we cross into the country

of the own-aware, possessing in perpetuity
this knowledge of number one *by number one*
no longer in escrow but available to be drawn

on for personal use—which might become
a burden in years remaining present
that father and mother cannot take back.

## Fabric to Mend

Atop the flannel sheets, atop the down-filled
comforter curves the caress of the night,
another layer to lull me to pleasant

sleep after another day's light has left
for destinations on the far side, some
of whose denizens' dreamtimes are ripped

and rent to blaze of bloodlight by missile
and other evils knived over the border
by a savage with satanic intent to scythe

peace to ribbons, allowing access to demons
all, whose claims are calamity and confrontation,
keeping at bay any blessed dark counterpane's drop

## Fugitive Relief

I claim sanctuary in the sacred
precinct of Friday night—

free from the coarse throats
that will clamor soon enough

on the other side of the night's holy wall.


Such a small shrine is this, a width
of only several hours in which I may

find the glow of solace and a span safe
from the rabble and its accusing maw

out there in Saturday's square where
echo even upon those free flagstones

the hoarse voices from the five-days
that tug and test the faith of those

pressed in working shifts to operate
far from the relics of the leisurely

saint that offer respite on that Eve,
whose expanse is a hymn to the turned

within and the sanct stillness of the lying-down.

## Blocks

Murder's just a mile from me but at least
bricks block bullets 'cause they can fly
many feet if unimpeded even in directions

distant from the target, just unintended
spray from an unconcerned finger
and unthinking mind, enough to dig

a divot in any nearby ground, green
or otherwise, or even softer skin all the way
through—rip and tear—to the empty other side

# Tour

Brother wine will accompany me
into a deep red evening, hours of elevation
above the average plain, a tethered balloon

from which to look down upon my usual self
—not in disdain—only a note of amusement
the distance allows, a perspective eagle-keen

the liquid lens grants me for this interval
of what I would not designate inebriation
but rather illumination, born of mild liquor

and its lift from any quotidian situation
to this exalted air, the source one glass,
clarity maintained by the ease of moderation.

## Charge Into

Edison's electrocution of the elephant
alliterates so appropriately—almost
an imitation of his DC current,
which would lose to Tesla and his AC,
lightning-powerful nonetheless,

but not so smooth on Topsy[1] the incorrigible
criminal offender (so said) who suffered
the primitive jolt, chained, smoked, and dropped
into death, heart seized up by the master's volts,
with his net of nerves like many more primates,

numb to the effect of electromagnetic magic,
conducting chains on an unknowing behemoth,
Coney Island amusement, in a new circuit
of hard energy, wiring the amped-up ages
soon to join our convenient, lethal grid.

---

1. Found in *Wikipedia*. Accessed 24 June 2022

## Framed Declaration

I thank father fish for my spine,
which with the earth allows me to align
and look straight up if I choose
into the sky in effort not to lose

my bearings and reconfirm my status
as one of capacity to focus on the stratus
and my semi-separation from the ground
rejoice in relative stability found

in the necessary inherited armature
support to compete with any furniture
remain myself and certainly discrete
while with lifetime gravity I must compete

## Simple Symposium

If Lot's wife were not a silent pillar of salt,
it would behoove her to get together

with Orpheus and compare notes
about that uncontrollable urge

to look back, which, I'm sure, he still
regrets and which she did at that seam

between animal—and mineral long since
washed away by millennia of rain

or the tongues of a million beasts seeking
in the desert dry and heat a rare lick—

> but forget those petrified by Medusa's
> puss for they were facing forward,

> with not forewarning, no chance to rue,
> no choice and thus no rubbering neck—

Let's keep this club for second thoughts,
if it could be, ruing the reality,

and rehashing what might have been

## Critical Eye

Quick—notice that this day is different
from the last—though the distinction

is difficult to discern. The subtle shade
is its own—*sui generis*—that will not

come again, the color is twenty-four hours
then no more despite any search for its match

in some enchiridion of infinite swatches
indexing the chances you might have seen

but did not distinguish if your eyes do not
hold the sensitive lens to split the micron

difference in the spectrum's strata adding
another every rising sun whose novelty

you should also note despite the static
scene within your purview as you rise

and repeat—but remember to reach
through the ostensible disguise—pull out

the face that is fresh and only hours old
but grows swiftly to yield to the next only one

# In Perpetuity

It is our old neighborhood despite the moves
of death and grown-up destinations
plus obvious additions and miscellaneous change
that veil the streets and yards from what is/was

death and grown-up destinations,
after all, are just temporary touches upon *our* thing,
that veil the streets and yards from what is/was
we know that which rests ever, under shallow paint

just temporary touches upon *our* thing
can only blind those who blink without memory's eye
we know that which rests ever, under shallow paint
peeling, flecking always evident to the sharp observer

only blind to those who blink without memory's eye
the ramshackle renovation or brand-spanking new
peeling, flecking always evident to the sharp observer
unlike we whose comfort lies in knowing the temporary dies,

the ramshackle renovation or brand-spanking new
is just window dressing for the upstart interlopers,
unlike we whose comfort lies in knowing the temporary dies—
it is our old neighborhood despite the moves.

## Former Integrity

Once there was a limit to heat's ingress,
a footstep non grata beyond the politeness

of the line *Natura* had arbitrated before we
were young, a land, if only in the mind's

ranging eye, to imagine cool retreat
from the tumult of the temperatures

rising as must go the tempers of our swarms
as we sweat in slick and sticky proximity

only pumping up the degrees and the attendant
*ira in illis diebus* that ended at the frontier

at least it was chill to think, but the border
floats, or even worse, recedes, and the tropic

tendrils creep up to some day of no retreat
and all too much steam and melting ice,

once a sign of solidity—no more, just the flow
upward whence we can only drop beads—go down

## Open Letter

Greetings to you whom I will never meet,
for most paths will never cross, so this

will be my substitute: hello, I hope you
are doing well and have—and will continue

into your future I will never see but may
imagine as a courtesy to your coming

experience and value of the life you will
lead totally without me or any awareness

of my living and acknowledgment of your
state, which unilateral lack does not trouble

me, as I am looking for no charity though
certainly would accept it if you ever deigned

to think about me in a fleeting feather
of attention whose tickle I might feel in one

of the places and years in which you and I
will remain ever unknown to each other and apart